Zefyr Lisowski's *Blood Box* is as much ouroboros as box, employing a circular structure to revisit the famous Fall River murders from alternating perspectives. Bookended by Lizzie Borden's voice, the collection shimmers with uncanniness as Lisowski channels the dead. The result is an exquisitely constructed *danse macabre* that shifts between reportage and invention, avowal and disavowal—an assembly of voices tethered together by a grisly loss. Moving us between the ghastliness of a father who "twisted the heads off pigeons" to the radiant beauty of a "pear tree's bright plumage," *Blood Box* is disturbing, dazzling, and riveting.
—**Simone Muench, author of *Wolf Centos, Orange Crush*, and with Dean Rader, *Suture***

BLOOD BOX

*Zefyr
Lisowski*

Black
Lawrence
Press

www.blacklawrence.com

Executive Editor: Diane Goettel
Chapbook Editor: Kit Frick
Book and Cover Design: Amy Freels
Cover art: "Untitled" (2013), from the body of work *The Precarious Weight of Ancestry*, by Tuesday Smillie. Used with permission.

Published 2019 by Black Lawrence Press.
Printed in the United States.

For my father
(1944–2017)

Contents

On the morning of August 4, 1892 in Fall River, MA, Lizzie Andrew Borden, thirty-two years of age, allegedly hacked her stepmother Abby and father Andrew to death with a hatchet (the weapon never found). Despite no other suspects emerging, Borden was acquitted of the crime June 30, 1893, living in Fall River with her sister Emma the rest of her life.

Ingredients for an Axe Girl

Insert girl.
Insert wet.
Insert family hurt axe hand.
Insert locks.

Make a box—kindness, hunger, etcetera.
Insert pear tree, juice dripping over the chin.
(Increase hunger. Increase doors.)

Insert tooth insert tooth insert tooth

She is lonely, and covered with blood.
Her flesh her body taut with thirties.
She is older.
Increase wealth. Increase grief.
I am not trying to build sympathy
but empty beds terrify me,
a thing howling and encrusted
outside the window. House like a coffin.
Decrease distance.

The summer heating like a firing chamber—
tender appearing in spurts as evaporated milk.

Questions appear:
Do you know the throng of cut, of bird?
Do you know this weight toward becoming?
What to do with all this unfurling—

Insert box, insert hand, insert blood box

If I Did

Lizzie

Then I must sleep in a sheet twisted
tight with blood, stomach heavy through the night.
Then I know the scream of the ferry.
Then "family" a word that stirs and stirs.
What use are doors in this weather? Of course

we hear everything—Father's moans ghost
through walls like cheesecloth. Here is a day.
       Here is another.
There's nothing to do but eat,
piling one plate then the next, pears
plummeting from the backyard brown as
blood. Father never
talks anymore, and Mrs. Borden
changes in my sleep to someone

who is still alive. We *always* lock our
rooms. My nightgown the finest terry cloth
or linen. Look at my face, my flushed cheek,
my lips. Look at my tenderness.

If I told you it was an intruder who did it,

would you take my hand in yours
and touch my trembling back?

It was. It was. Oh God, it was.

The Prosecution Examines Lizzie, August 22, 1892

I. Can you describe your settings and early life,
if you will, and the state of Fall River at the time
of the murders, please, of Andrew and Abby
Borden, and give a complete history of your mind
at the time of finding of the bodies of your father
and stepmother, without holding out any prurient
details, please, or statements of incrimination.

II. Can you elaborate on that, please,
not obscuring or eluding any of the facts.

III. Did you know of anyone your father was
on bad terms with, please.

IV. You have been on pleasant terms with your
stepmother since the incident of which you speak,
have you made any efforts to find the person on
bad terms with aforementioned.

V. That morning, had you any knowledge of her
going out the house. I repeat, and hope I need not
repeat the question further.

VI. I repeat.

VII. I shall ask you once more about that morning.

VIII. I repeat again.

IX. Miss Borden, of course you appreciate the anxiety
that everybody has to find the author of this tragedy,
and the questions that I put to you have been
in that direction; I now ask you if you can furnish
any other fact, please, or give any other,
even suspicion, that will assist the officers in any way
in this matter?

X. Have you sealskin sacks?

XI. I repeat the question.

Sunday Mass, April 12, 1891

Lizzie

In church, our lips move silently to the hymns.
By lips, I mean: our throats. The whispers
here are so mean, Father
tormented by his pettiness.
By our, I mean: Mrs. Borden.
By our, I mean: my father.
By our, I mean: me.
Don't absolve me of this.
I am in the pews, singing
the songs like they are his body,
and I am fourteen again—
still learning how to keep a secret,
turn the lock on a bedroom door.
Don't absolve me of this.
By throats, I mean as follows:
last week I taught at the mission,
same as any other. Children
surrounded me as I held up the flimsy
paperback, pointed to the illustration

of Christ in the garden. My voice
felt aflame, as if I couldn't say
the words I had planned.
But they came out anyway:
This is what it means to feel,
I said, pointing at His tears.
His fingers are so rough.
This is what it means to feel alone.

Inquest Testimony, August 12, 1892

Lizzie

The day before the murders my uncle visits, seeped
in dust from the cattle farms out West.

Face bristled, muscled arms bulging. The maid—
who Emma and I call *Maggie* though her name is really *Bridget*—
picks up his sullied bowler from the hook he flings it onto.

Over dinner, he tells us: "Iowa is a venerable baptism!" And:
"I feel reborn by the work!" He asks for $1,000. Maggie
watches from the eaves—Mrs. Borden handles the cooking

on nights with company, so the maid hides
herself, avoids Father's
hatchet face and shadow. She corners me

after dinner, asks again to leave—"it's not the work
that's the problem," she says, "it's the dreams."
Do I feel pity? Of course I say

nothing, but in private I hoped to sit her down, hold her
hand, tell my own visions. The trees dying

in the heat. Red splattering everything.
And moving toward the front door,

a dream, I lose myself. Entering our home
like an omen, it emerges: a husk

of person who looks like all of us,
but acts like us as well.

Fall River Herald Reportage, August to September 1892

That might account for the blood stains on the axes.

Their friends admit that things were not as pleasant as they might have been in that house.

Seven out of the nine stories that were reported to the police were investigated, and all were found to be myth.

There was no man lurking within the chimney.

Mrs. Borden was not the mother of the girls, and the father was not overly liberal with them.

The funeral services took place at eleven o'clock and were strictly private.

Some stories that have been written about these relations should be regarded as the grossest exaggeration.

A blossom of bone flower, spreading over her face—

The door was found open after the murders, and it appears that no one saw Mrs. Borden for two hours.

Miss Lizzie says she spent the morning of the tragedy in the barn, eating pears.

The bodies were not moved, tho they were horrible to look at.

Each head crushed like grape—

They found no hidden chambers—

The remaining family shaken by the events [...] have been prescribed morphine liberally—

The pear tree's bright plumage—

That afternoon, all that matched the searchers' gaze were boxes of clothing—

The Maid Speaks, October 10, 1892
Bridget

And they do keep me in their meanness

    And I am not safe

And this summer so hot—

    I am molting everyone is.

Do you see the sheets crisping in the wind

Do you see the feathers, falling still from

every single tree

Yes I saw the bodies

Who didnt

Visiting the Bordens, August 2, 1892

John V. Morse

I'm talking about being possessed by something.
Back out West, we called it *heat lightning.* Here,
something else. Maybe *fester*? I have a man—
he breeds the cattle and I sell them. At night,
he wraps his arms around me like garters.
I miss my house—scrabble of a roof, dewdrops
at night and lizards in morning—more and more
each day of this terrible trip. I miss your sweet lips,
scratch of bristle. Do you have the same longings?
Here, there are just walls inside walls,
stepsibling Andrew's petty study. Quiet Emma.
And strange Lizzie, who seems bound by a box
of its own sort—a feeling, I must confess, not
entirely foreign to me, either. Now. Here.

Dear Mother, February 10, 1890
Bridget

They dont trust me but they pay me—

Mother I hope that is good enough.

Enclosed a small coin purse,

fabric   all I get

at the moment   Everything else

goes to savings   or

Our Redeemer   Communion

wine is sweet in Fall

River, and when I swallow

I think of you

Tell me the reverse is true—

Tell me you are well Mother

Wish me health

    and kindness

        and safety

Keep me well

I miss you terribly

    Yr daughter Bridget

Poem in Which Nothing Happens, August 3, 1892

Lizzie

First, an ache. Then, click of fingers on latches. I never write about my sister Emma, who is never at ease in this maze, I mean house, I mean spite. She says, *we have walls to keep secrets, and locks to hold them tight.* Father is away most days. Our home looks like this regularly:

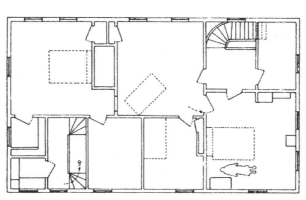

but in my dreams it's even more monstrous, walls bent like a crust of whalebone. I will be thirty-two, which also is a type of box. I walk the thin floors of my bedroom every day, hearing the bicker and creak of the house. The only relief we have is supper—another geometry, another violence too.

There's been a death. Of course no one knows what to do (August 10, 1892)

Emma

My brow is thick, my hands heavy. I redraw
my face every day in this tumescent heat—hoping

for an almost showy sadness. I am nothing compared to my
sister. Journalists say "remorseless" to describe her rouged
visage. As if painting only exists to create new emotions.
As if kindness were an aesthetic choice.

If there was anything Mrs. Borden knew, it was that—the way she buried those garden pears
    inside her pies.
Face powdered into blankness. How can any of us

compete with *her* secrets? I tell Lizzie, *of course she knew
what we said of her.* She knew everything:

how molasses covers up the festering sweet
of rot. Makeup, lockbox, little hole
in the ground. Grief is made

by its performance. Am I bereaved?

Look at me: I wear

my suffering on my skin. I wear my skin
on top of my other skin.

Preparing for the Wedding Anniversary, June 5, 1890
Abby

Why wouldn't I have heard the rumors?

When Andrew proposed (they say), it was with a ring fetched from a dead man.

Of course I realized I was wed to an undertaker—anyone could see his face, stretched taut as a morgue sheet.

Tenderness wasn't what I was looking for.

The house we live in sweats like a human.

But the sound of his feet thumping the stairs, or his face in the heat, that's something else entirely.

The pear tree, its fecundity of pears.

We sleep in a narrow bed, and I dream of him in embrace, spread out like a lover or thin patty of flesh.

Sketches for a Family Portrait, August 1, 1892

Lizzie

Is all this grief repetitive to you?

I see my stepmother and look at a straw creature.

I see my uncle, fresh from the long expanse

of Iowa,

and there are only shadows, heaps of luggage.

I'm spending more and more time in the barn—

its stifle, scratch and warp of floor. From there,

I can see the plyboard of our home, plump droop of

pear tree. Violence dances with us like ghosts. Uncle John's

voice booming over our evening meal. This family

filthens me. When trying to escape, I close

my eyes and think of Massachusetts' rocky

coast—which I've only seen once, its seaboard

a slate as silver-grey as my father's dry eyes. Its shore

salty as the coat he hangs up grimed

by the completion of each day's errands.

This is our intimacy, the bond we keep:

I always pass by before he climbs the back stairs.

I am careful to avoid eye contact.

He is careful to keep the door locked afterward.

Finding the Pigeons, July 29, 1892
Lizzie

A bundle of broken wings from the barn,
blood staining the stoop.

"They were making too much noise," Father says.

I cover the bird bodies, wretched necks,
     with a piece of gingham.

I don't weep.

Body Wrench

Emma

When I am burgled, I know what happens—
Our walls are so thin. Our skins are also walls.
Flesh and house both a thing that steals.
Her eyes like teeth.

I wrench my body in my sleep,
I dream of it slithering past, I vow
the following: abandon you.
My sister. My stepmother. A thorn.
Who else is in this list.

When I am burgled, I wait
for it to happen again:

my abandonment will be floral,
can never go out.

I ask questions to the house—

Do you ever feel kindness
or warmth, can your flowers bloom

I don't

They don't

Celebrating Another Anniversary, June 6, 1891
Abby

A year past our twenty-fifth anniversary, Andrew's face settles into a finer granite, boney as the roast I am cooking him for our occasion.

I wait until Emma and Lizzie are out of the house before I serve the food—

someone burgled us of late, and I give no kindness to his children, make them a bed of indifference,

because that was what Andrew showed me in the aftermath. How
to lay a hand with heaviness, keep secrets

in the back of the kitchen where no one looks. The sutures, coffin nails, buried fishing weights that hold a family together.

I am so tired. Andrew smacking his lips constantly, eyes roving through the house.

Even before the robbery, I sleep like an ex-lover, wake up panicked and afraid.

I reheat the food. I avoid the daughters when they call.

Church, October 12, 1890

Emma

Do I believe in a God? Of course I do.
I pray daily—sometimes at First Church,

sometimes Central Congregational Universal
Blood of Christ. I make my bedroom a place

of sanctity. I'm a good Christian.
I pray for fresh fruit, an end to the heat. I

never expect a reply. The God I know
lives behind a locked door and only hoards

His good things. If He has children,
He beats them without fail. If He has neighbors,

He chops apart their houses. Tell me,
who wouldn't believe. My father emerges

from the study and only speaks to the maid,
or his grubby wife, or my sister. I'm in constant

pain. The minister says, "God is all around us."
Tell me. Who could require more proof than that.

A Corrective, July 12, 1891
Abby

I talk about Andrew because it's how I've been taught—

The safety in men against the curl of sin in my breast,

crinoline I use to cover where the bruises show.

I try so hard to be disciplined, Godly, a "good" "woman." But young

Emma tells me when I move in of her mother, her mother's

rage their inheritance, her mother haunts me. Dead

Sarah, Emma says, shadows Lizzie, fingers more a wolf's

than a woman's. I don't look for ghosts, I only talk to Andrew.

   But my second

week in the house I find a letter, unsigned, in the boudoir:

"were she still alive, she would kill you immediately." Neither

Borden girl says a word, but that, too, a reason I've turned

to my man, sought comfort in he who brought me to this grave:

face spiteful, his knobbed spine a rock I cling to against all else.

Forgiveness only means that which we can or cannot forget.

Talking to the Priest, August 6, 1892

Emma

Before he died, I asked him to send a letter,
and he did. She was never as charitable, but
even still: the week before presented me with

a thin gold band. *Reward for the Lord's work,*
Abby said, and I wept. I kept my own schedule,
ate meals alone from the both of them, and

spent that whole wretched summer traveling
as my sister was teaching church. I see her
rereading the same poor pages—

*Stories of New England. The Wide, Wide World.
The Book of Common Prayer.* We talked to family
only through formalities. It's that last thing

that stays in my mind even now—what caused
me to reach out to you, Pastor. Surely you can
understand this hell I'm in? How the hating

and the missing can only arrive together. The way
my parents' absence, just as their presence,
remains the same dull ache.

Eating the Pears, Fall 1892

Lizzie

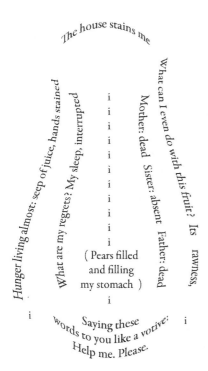

The house stains me

i
i
i
i
i
i
i
i
i

(Pears filled
and filling
my stomach)

i

Hunger living almost: seep of juice, hands stained

What are my regrets? My sleep, interrupted

Mother: dead   Sister: absent   Father: dead

What can I even do with this fruit?   Its   rawness,

i

Saying these
words to you like a votive:
Help me. Please.

i

Body Wrench
Emma

And suddenly, it unhappens.

10:05 a.m., August 4, 1892
Lizzie

What are you expecting? My hands
and the axe's head? It's late morning, the sun red
outside, thick stew of air

running through every building I'm in.
The barn is hot.
Weeks ago, father twisted the heads off pigeons
roosting here, where I am—they
were not my pigeons, it was not even my barn. This
is not motive or confession,

my flesh as thick that day as any other.
My pulse elevated, wretched
with ghost grief—it's morning,

and Abby's climbing the stairs to put the fresh sheets on the guest bed.

I am here. I am not here. The house,
this cage,

Abby is thinking things like: *I am a regretful woman.*
Or: *I will change my life.*
Or, she is thinking
nothing, mind blank as sheets spreading over bedframe.

Father has a poker body,
his favoring of me a mutability.

She is creasing the pillows, work that Bridget would never do.
Bridget.

Emma's absence a blood box.
My love for her.

Do you know the worst part of an act. Its regret.

She is almost out of the bedroom—

The past few months bolster me in their heat. Sheness
shedding across the yard. Do I litter underneath
the incessant summer moon? Am I
a non-compliant daughter,
        I am barely a daughter,
I am trying to comply, self slipping out of my wet hands—

self an oven—

I have, of course, regrets and more regrets.
Look at all of them.
A fountain, bubbling into carpet rot. The seep
of floorboards.

That morning,
I cry,

I count my love for her.

The house creaks.

The house says, *Look,*
        there is nothing between us—

What are you expecting? A reward? A triumph? There's nothing in this story
but pain—

My hands bruised red, scratch of my father's shirtcuffs tearing me
to pieces.

I am familiar with pieces.

A sudden call
of bird.

Look at she climbing the stairs
to the guest room.

I count all my love.

The head so severely battered, no pictures of its face exist to this day.

Dusting the Guest Bed, August 4, 1892, 10:00 a.m.
Abby

Guilt needles into

each of us, he says, *consider practicing*

forgiveness. I trust my pastor so make

myself make a series of tasks:

cook dinner, set beds, collect rags.

My hands worn. My stepchildren

in their place. Help me, Lord, with

this seeking forgiveness. Mouth

it in me like an echo. Grace

can come sudden and I almost hear you,

distant as a footstep, climbing

first the stairway, then the landing,

then pausing thick

and breathy at my neck. I can

be kinder. Can I be kinder?

Lord, I believe. I am sorry

and the bed is almost made. Say

it to me again: *I can change.*

Of course, of course,

of course I can change.

The Sheets, January 9, 1893

Lizzie

I'm well aware of my failings—temper like a brick,
thick, quarrelsome ribs. I am building a body

out of other bodies, my sins haunted by other sins. Maybe
the word I'm looking for is a feeling instead:

the way jurors ogle at me when I enter
the courtroom, red paint still splashed bright

on my doorstep. Body brimming with brim.
      This isn't new—even much younger,

my conduct stains everything around. When I touch
my traveling companion, she doesn't recoil until the following

day. When I put my lips over hers,
she responds in turn. All my life, I've dealt with the weight

of my actions, and that night, twined together,
my father's face

enters my dreams,
smashed like a cantaloupe.

Her breath warm against my babycheeks,
skin pillowy, sweet. Listen, if I've

learnt anything, I learnt it many times:
every person who's seen, then unseen me,

across my path. Her guilty face
when she realizes what

we've done. All of my she's.
        The men are

deliberating, fingers willowy
 and oh so many coats.

        Inside the courtroom,

body splayed against the stand,
time is still passing.

What answers do they even want
but me punished.

Who hasn't tried to lose themselves
in their own body.

These men, their rules.

I can still hear the ferry.

Body Wrench
Emma

We wear black veils to the funeral
and the coffins hold light like a basket.

It is August. Our clothes swelter.
The trees that line their plot are unsavory.

I do not cry and do not sleep.

Beneath the clothes, my body is falling
apart, becoming illuminated

with flame,

and they are not here:

I do not grieve
I do not grieve

If I Didn't

Lizzie

"Not guilty" holds meanings in its skin too,
and I am deeply acquainted with all of them—
a series of cells dancing between my eyes,
fingers corpsing on the table, the investigator
peeling wallpaper from the parlor. I'm used
to others' stares, their pauses. I'm used to silence.
Am I haunted? I am haunted. Even in the courtroom,
as they mouth the acquittal, I start dreaming
of another life—surely I can find happiness. I know
this because I ignore my dreams, and eat food
regularly. I know this because I've read stories,
miraculous instances of angelic visitations,
shipwrecks that reverse themselves, a fire that,
suddenly, stops burning. Do you see it? Kindness
flocking like birds? I'm talking about a forgiveness
so close to touching you, you can taste it—

there it is, the yard over.
There it is, climbing the fence.

There it is, raising thin hand to rap,
delicately,
at the parlor door.

Answer it.

Notes & Acknowledgments

Gratitude to the following journals who first published poems from *Blood Box*, sometimes in earlier forms:

DIAGRAM; *The Texas Review*; *Action, Spectacle*; *Jet Fuel Review*; and *Verse.Press*.

*　　*　　*

"The Prosecution Examines Lizzie" is composed from interview questions during the August 1892 preliminary trial.

"*Fall River Herald* Reportage" is composed, mainly, from articles in the *Fall River Herald,* August-November 1892.

"Sketches for a Family Portrait, August 1, 1892" owes a structural debt to Donika Kelly's "Fourth Grade Autobiography."

"Bone flower" is a phrase borrowed from Robert Hayden's "Bone-Flower Elegy."

Most historical notes sourced from the primary documents housed at lizzieandrewborden.com or in *The Lizzie Borden Sourcebook* (Brandon, 1992).

*   *   *

Thanks deeply to everyone who helped me write this book, talked with me about it, contributed in some way, or offered me food and support over the past two years. I'm sure I'm leaving folks out.

Nadia Cheney, Rami Karim, Geo Holly, Phoebe Glick, Chase Berggrun, Robin Reid Drake, Kat Cheairs, Kerry Downey, Maren Beam, Joey de Jesus, Muriel Leung, Alexandra Watson, the rest of the Apogee family, Eddie Emma (thanks for the bereavement sweater), Brandon Covington Sam-Sumana, Charles Theonia, Raquel Salas Rivera, Rax King, Jen Fitzgerald, Renata Lisowski, Buzz Slutzky, Jesse Rice-Evans, Donna Masini, Candace Thompson, Tuesday Smillie, Valentine Conaty, Ching-In Chen, Tracy May Fuad, Madeleine Walker, Simone Muench, Mariam Bazeed, Katie Jean Shinkle. My editor Kit Frick, and the rest of the folks at Black Lawrence Press. My therapist. My mom. My coterie of exes.

My dad's shadow is over everything.

And thanks, of course, to Lizzie.

*   *   *

The *Untitled* diptych on the cover of *Blood Box* comes from a body of works by Tuesday Smillie titled *The Precarious Weight of Ancestry*. These works, consisting of watercolor drawings and collage, consider the sometimes intangible, sometimes amorphous presence of familial inheritance. They reference a tangle of histories and social locations, including race and class, as well as legacies of creativity and bad mental health. *The Precarious Weight of Ancestry* engages an abstracted presence of this inheritance, ever present, but rarely directly acknowledged (particularly by those in positions of relative privilege). The narratives built around this inheritance attempt, and fail, to produce cohesive meaning. For Smillie, *The Precarious Weight of Ancestry* resonates simultaneously as a gift and threat; a cloud of smoke, a picture (puzzle) unresolved.

For more on *The Precarious Weight of Ancestry* and Smillie's artwork, visit TuesdaySmillie.com

Zefyr Lisowski also goes by Zef and is a queer poet, artist, and Southern transplant currently based in New York. She's a poetry co-editor for *Apogee Journal*, an instructor at Hunter College, and is also author of the micro-chapbook *Wolf Inventory* (Ghost City Press, 2018). Zef's received support from the Tin House Summer Workshop, the New York Live Arts Fest, and Sundress Academy for the Arts, among other places; her work has appeared in *Muzzle Magazine*, *DIAGRAM*, *Entropy*, *The Texas Review*, and elsewhere. She is a 2018 Pushcart nominee.

Photo: NM.Esc